EYEWITNESS

DOG

Great Dane
puppies
Bloodhound
Red fox
Skeleton of
maned wolf
French bulldog
Lurcher

EYEWITNESS

DOG

Written by
JULIET CLUTTON-BROCK

Australian terrier

King Charles spaniel

Doberman pinscher

Bernese mountain dog

Arctic fox cub in summer

REVISED EDITION

DK DELHI
Senior Editor Rupa Rao
Senior Art Editor Vikas Chauhan
Project Art Editor Heena Sharma
Editor Deeksha Micek
Team Lead, Picture Research Sumedha Chopra
Deputy Manager, Picture Research Virien Chopra
Deputy Managing Editor Sreshtha Bhattacharya
Managing Editor Kingshuk Ghoshal
Managing Art Editor Govind Mittal
Pre-production Designer Pawan Kumar
Pre-production Image Editor Jagtar Singh
Project Jackets Art Editor Vidushi Chaudhry
Creative Head Malavika Talukder

DK LONDON
Senior Editor Georgina Palffy
Art Editor Chrissy Checketts
US Senior Editor Megan Douglass
Managing Editor Francesca Baines
Managing Art Editor Philip Letsu
Production Editor Dragana Puvacic
Production Controller Jack Matts
Publisher Andrew Macintyre
Art Director Mabel Chan

Consultants James Conroy, Debra M. Eldredge

FIRST EDITION
Project Editor Marion Dent
Art Editor Jutta Kaiser-Atcherley
Senior Editor Helen Parker
Senior Art Editor Julia Harris
Special Photography Jerry Young, Alan Hills of the British Museum, Colin Keates of the Natural History Museum

This Eyewitness ® Guide has been conceived by Dorling Kindersley Limited and Editions Gallimard

This American Edition, 2025
First American Edition, 1991
Published in the United States by DK Publishing, a division of Penguin Random House LLC
1745 Broadway, 20th Floor, New York, NY 10019

25 26 27 28 29 10 9 8 7 6 5 4 3 2 1
001-350873-Dec/2025

Published in Great Britain by Dorling Kindersley Limited
ISBN 978-0-5939-7216-8 (Paperback)
ISBN 979-8-2171-2536-4 (ALB)

Printed and bound in China

www.dk.com

This book was made with Forest Stewardship Council™ certified paper—one small step in DK's commitment to a sustainable future.
Learn more at www.dk.com/uk/information/sustainability

Azara's fox

Skull of fennec fox

Cross-bred dog

Miniature pinscher

Chinese lion dog figurine

Raccoon dog in winter coat

Spanish greyhound

Jack Russell terrier

Contents

Boxer

What is a **dog?**

The dog family (Canidae) includes about 35 species, such as wolves, jackals, foxes, and wild dogs. Domestic dogs are descended from a now-extinct subspecies of gray wolves. Canids are omnivores, with traits for hunting: their teeth slice through meat with ease. They rely on their sharp senses of sight, hearing, and smell to find prey. Domestic dogs typically mate twice a year. After two months in the womb, pups are born blind and deaf, and depend on their mother for survival.

DISTRIBUTION OF DOGS

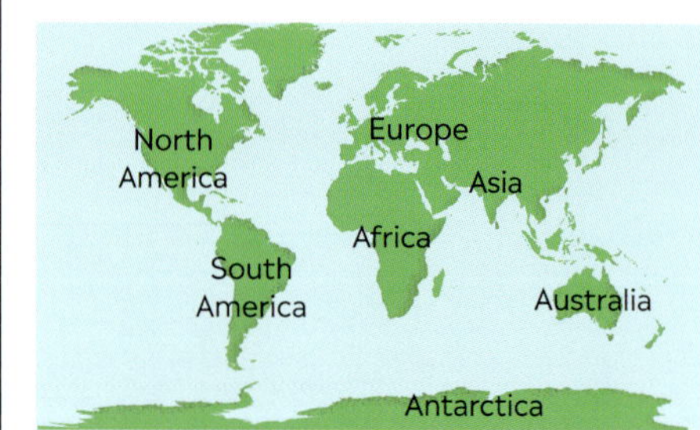

Wild canids originally lived in every continent of the world except for Antarctica and Australia where they were introduced by humans.

Doggies of all sorts

Dogs come in all shapes, sizes, and colors. More than 400 breeds of domestic dog (pp. 48-61) are descended from a subspecies of the gray wolf.

Coat is multicolored and distinctive.

African hunting dog

Ears are small, erect, and rounded.

Jovial jackals

There are three species of jackal (pp. 24–25)—the golden, the side-striped, and the black-backed. They all live in Africa; the golden jackal is found also in Europe and Asia.

Golden jackal

Red fox

Solitary hunter

The red fox hunts rabbits and rodents on its own. The behavior of foxes (pp. 28–31) differs from other canids (pp. 18–19). All foxes have a bushy tail.

Warm feet

Dogs have long made good foot warmers. This medieval stained glass depicts the biblical characters Tobias and Sarah—and their dog.

When a pack of wolves howls, it can be heard from
10 miles (16 km) away.

Teeth usually number 42 (p. 9).

Gray wolf

Wolves' thick fur can be nearly pure white, red, brown, gray, or black.

African hunting dog

This social wild dog (p. 26) hunts in family groups in the African grasslands. It is in danger of extinction from disease and conflict with farmers due to encroachment on each other's land.

The largest canid

The gray wolf (pp. 22–23) is the largest living wild canid and the closest relative of all domestic dogs. It lives and hunts in a pack.

What is not a dog?

Hyenas, Tasmanian wolves (now extinct), and prairie dogs are not dogs. Hyenas are closer to cats. The Tasmanian wolf was a marsupial (pouched mammal) in Australia. The North American prairie dog is a rodent.

Rounded ears

Tasmanian wolf

It may have looked like a dog but the Tasmanian wolf was a marsupial and unrelated to the dog family. It is now known only from stuffed specimens in museums.

Hyena

The striped hyena is a hunter and scavenger in Africa and western Asia.

Dog family **evolution**

Fossil evidence shows that the ancestors of modern dogs first appeared in Eurasia and North America. One of the earliest genera, *Hesperocyon,* lived in North America between 40 and 37 million years ago. In Eurasia, *Cynodictis*, which lived around 35 million years ago, is considered to be an early canid-like carnivore. Over time, these species evolved into more specialized canids, eventually leading to the species we see today.

Dogs in space

The bright Dog Star (Sirius) in the constellation *Canis Major* evolved some 200 million years before the first dogs.

Dire consequences

The extinct dire wolf lived in California during the Ice Age. It was huge and preyed on horses, bison, and some other smaller mammals.

***Cynodictis* is also called a bear dog because it looks like a cross between the two.**

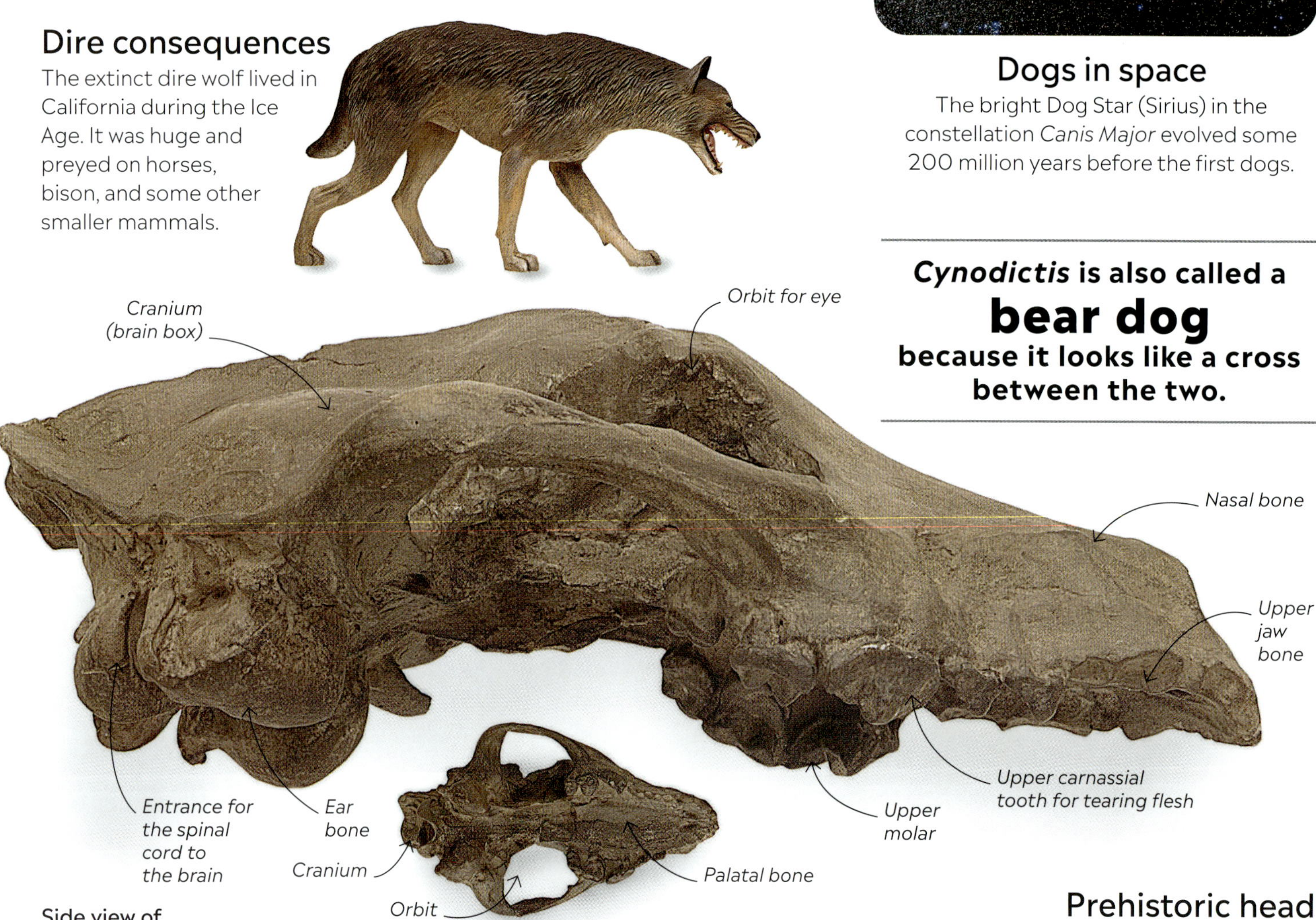

Side view of *Cynodictis* skull

Inside view of *Cynodictis* skull

Prehistoric head

This is a 30-million-year-old fossilized skull of one of the early dog family ancestors—the doglike animal called *Cynodictis*.

EYEWITNESS

Angela Perri
American archaeologist Dr. Angela Perri studies prehistoric dog remains with a focus on interaction between people and dogs. Perri and her team study the genetics of ancient dogs in sites around the world to find out about the domestication of early canines.

Incisor for gripping, biting, and tearing meat from bone

Premolar for reducing food to small pieces

Upper carnassial (4th premolar) for cutting flesh and bone

Upper canine for gripping and killing prey

Lower carnassial (1st molar)

Side view of wolf skull

Wild canid

Like most canids, a wolf has 42 teeth: 12 incisors, 4 canines, 16 premolars, and 10 molars (4 upper, 6 lower).

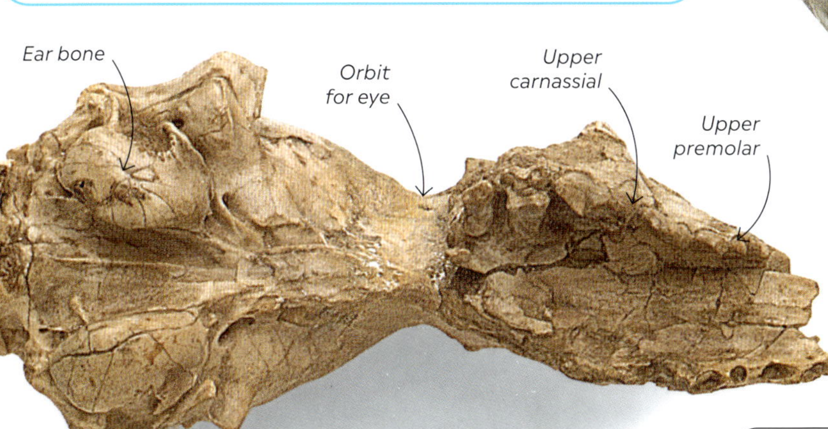

Palatal (roof of mouth) view of *Tomarctus* skull

Very distant relative

The fossil skull shows the roof of the mouth of the *Tomarctus*. Not closely related to dog family ancestors, it lived in North Africa until five million years ago.

Illustration of a *Hyaenodon* next to an animal carcass by the German artist Heinrich Harder

Not an old hyena

Hyaenodon was larger than most carnivores of its time. It lived in North America and Eurasia until around 23 million years ago. It had a large head and powerful jaws, but is not an ancestor of today's hyenas.

MODERN EVOLUTION

During the last Ice Age, wolves and humans lived as family groups of social hunters, competing for the same prey. A select few wolf cubs were tamed. This interaction may have contributed to the early stages of the domestication of dogs, which took place over thousands of years.

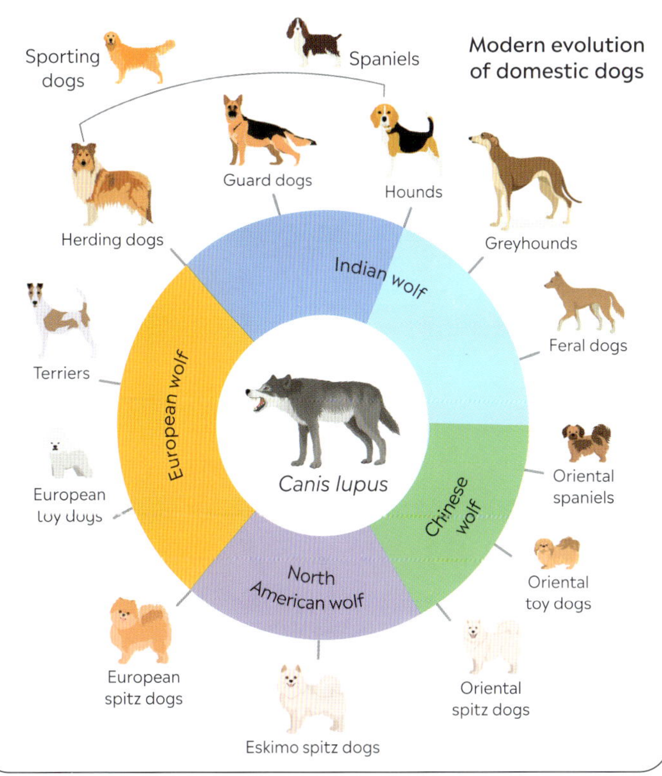

Modern evolution of domestic dogs

Dogs' **bones**

A mammal's skeleton provides the body's framework, protecting and supporting key organs and allowing the body to move. Bones are joined together at joints, and cord-like ligaments hold the bones in place. Tendons are the elastic tips that connect muscles to the bones; muscles contract and relax to move the body in all directions. Each canid bone is characteristic of the dog family: the skulls of wolves, dogs, and foxes are long with large teeth; the neck and backbone are long; the rib cage protects the chest; and the long limb bones are adapted for fast running.

Large tearing, or carnassial, tooth

Arctic wolf

Top size

Among wild canids, wolves have the largest skeleton.

Neck vertebrae

Sternum

Elbow joint

Radius

Ulna

Skeleton of African hunting dog

African hunter

The African hunting dog (p. 6) has very long legs in relation to its body size, so is able to roam far for prey.

African hunting dog

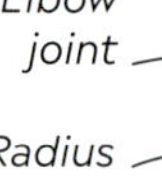

Little red

The red fox creeps under rocks and bushes. Its legs are short in comparison to its long body.

Red fox

Pelvis

Tibia

Radius

Elbow joint

Ulna

Ankle joint, or hock

Skeleton of red fox

Lower jaw

Shoulder joint

Sternum

Metacarpal bone

Skeleton of Maltese dog

Round skull

Maltese dog

Ball of fluff

This Maltese dog doesn't look like a wolf, but its skeleton is built like one. However, dogs bred for different tasks typically have skeletons that differ in shape and build.

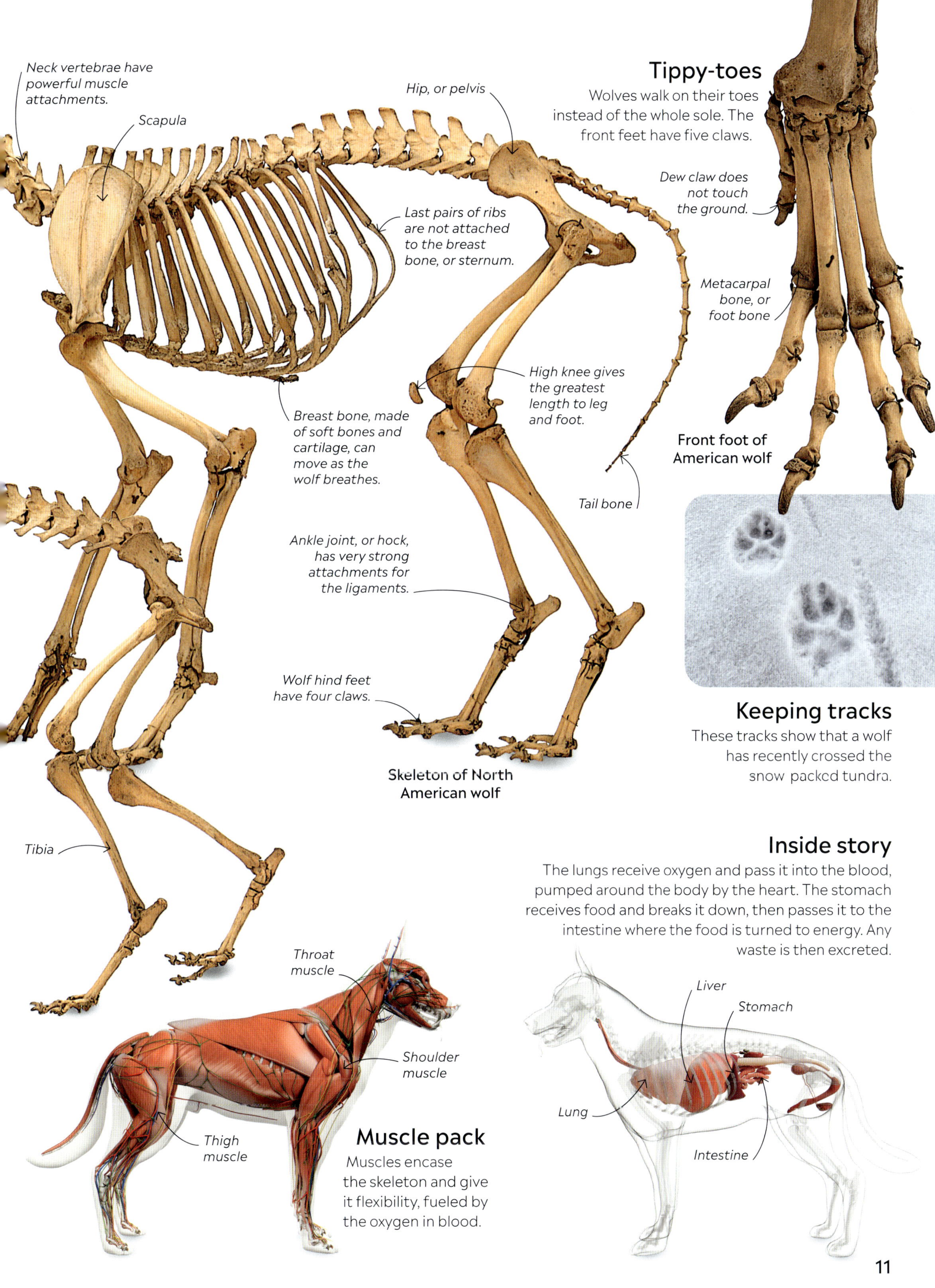

Skeleton of North American wolf

Tippy-toes

Wolves walk on their toes instead of the whole sole. The front feet have five claws.

Front foot of American wolf

Keeping tracks

These tracks show that a wolf has recently crossed the snow packed tundra.

Inside story

The lungs receive oxygen and pass it into the blood, pumped around the body by the heart. The stomach receives food and breaks it down, then passes it to the intestine where the food is turned to energy. Any waste is then excreted.

Muscle pack

Muscles encase the skeleton and give it flexibility, fueled by the oxygen in blood.

Coats, **heads, tails**

Fur keeps dogs warm. It is dense in cold climates, but short in hot ones. Some breeds have two layers of fur: a fine wool undercoat, usually of one color; and a top coat of longer, coarser hairs with natural oils to make it waterproof, and a striped (brindled) fur pattern. All wild dog heads are long with erect ears, and teeth set in a line along straight jaws. Tails are used for balance, expressing feelings, and signaling.

Tail tales

Dog tails can be straight, curly, fluffy, or smooth. In the past, tails of some breeds would be docked (cut off) for cosmetic reasons or to prevent injury. This painful practice is now illegal in many countries, but may still be performed by a vet on some breeds of working dog.

Coat varieties

Coat colors are variations of white, black, and tan. Dogs with two layers of hairs can have striped (brindled) fur patterns. Most dogs molt in spring and fall, so they have a thin coat in summer and a thick one in winter.

Round face

Japanese chins (a breed of spaniel) have little, round heads and short, curved jaws.

Long or short?

While some dog breeds have the long, narrow faces of their wolfish ancestors, others have been bred selectively to have short, broad faces. As a result, some dog breeds today show no physical resemblance to wolves.

Arctic wolf

Side view of Japanese chin skull

Bloodhound

Bat-eared fox

Fox terrier

Side view of skull of bat-eared fox

Pekingese

Toothy fox

The bat-eared fox has four to eight more teeth than any other canid, but they are smaller.

Sight, **sound**

Domestic dogs have inherited their sight and hearing ability from the wolf. These senses evolved to fit a social hunter of large prey, later developing through "selective breeding" into modern-day dogs. For example, in sight hounds (pp. 48–49), puppies with good sight were chosen as breeders, so, over time, the hounds developed even better sight. In the wild, wolves and dogs hunt at dusk, when sight is important. Foxes hunt at night, when hearing is more important.

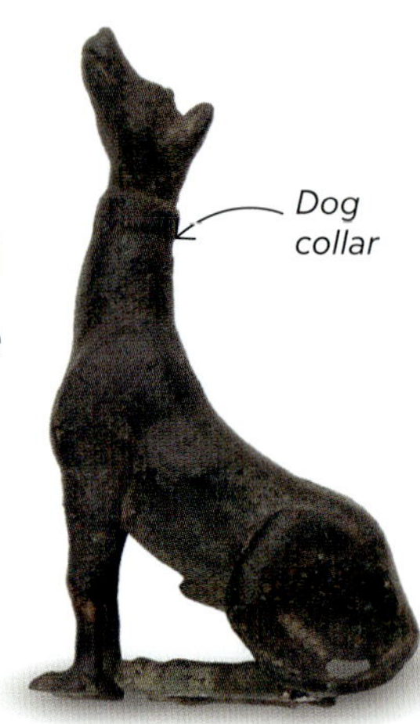

Guard dog

This ancient Roman sculpture shows a dog watching and listening for intruders.

Listen up

The large, erect ears are turned each way as the dog figures out where the sound is coming from.

THE EAR

All wild dogs have erect ears to help them tell where a sound has come from.

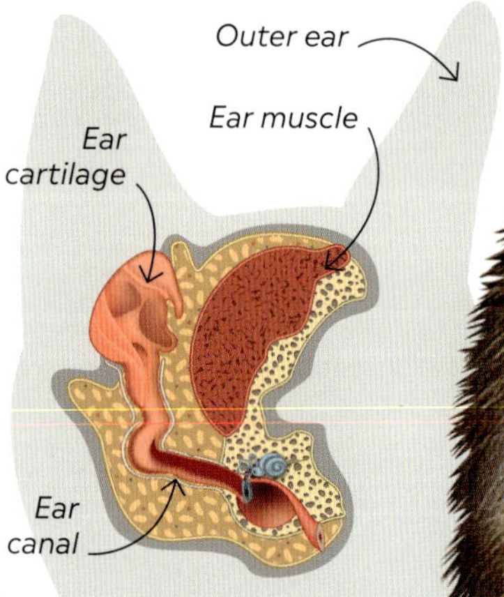

Outer ear

Ear muscle

Ear cartilage

Ear canal

Dog whistle

Most dogs will respond to the sound of a whistle.

Dense fur keeps a fennec fox warm on cold nights in the desert.

Huge ears help a fennec fox keep cool and hear any sound.

Belly fur is even paler, as it is on nearly every carnivore.

Fur is pale to reflect daytime heat.

Fennec fox

This smallest fox family member lives in the desert. It is adapted for keeping cool and finding food in the sand.

THE EYE
Dogs have a third eyelid, which protects the eye from dirt and dust.
Upper eyelid
Pupil
Iris
Third eyelid, or nictitating membrane
Lower eyelid
Beautiful borzoi
The borzoi is a sight, or "gaze," hound. With keen sight, it was once used in game and wolf hunts.
Some borzoi have snouts more than 12 in (30 cm) long.
Deep chest tapers down to a narrow waist.
Efficient hunter
Keen eyesight, a streamlined body, and long legs make the greyhound an excellent hunter. It also has the ability to instinctively focus on its prey.
Greyhound

On the **scent**

Pointer pointing

A pointer ranges over the ground with its keen nose and then "points" out the game.

Most canids have an acute sense of smell, which is essential for hunting, finding mates, and recognizing others in their territory. This is made possible by the nasal cavity, which is highly adapted to process scents. While scent is the dominant sense in many species, some, such as the bat-eared fox, rely more on their hearing to detect prey. Certain hunting dogs have been bred to have an acute sense of smell.

Who are you?

A dog can learn a lot by smelling the anal gland of another dog.

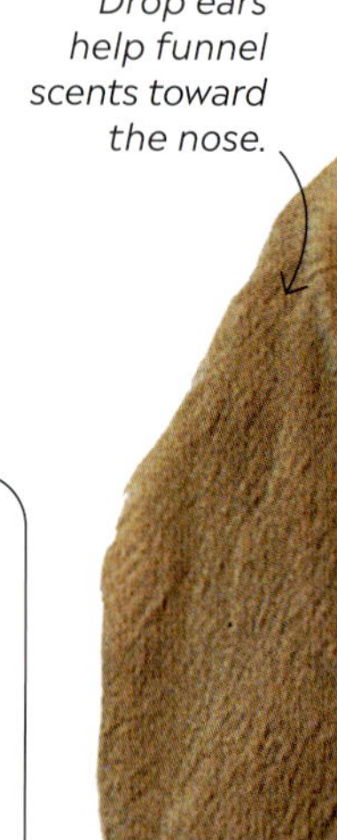

Drop ears help funnel scents toward the nose.

NASAL CAVITY

Scent particles are drawn over rolls of fine bone in the nasal cavity. From here, nerves message the brain.

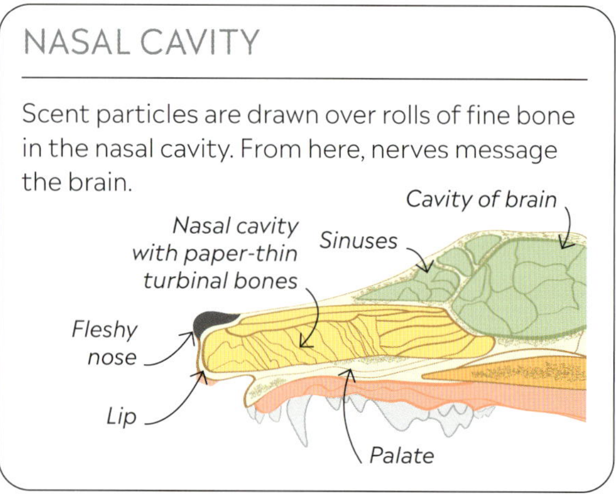

Dachshund's nose

All the dog family have leathery noses and two nostrils, which draw scents into the nasal cavity.

The bat-eared fox relies less on its nose and more on its exceptional hearing to detect prey.

Bat-eared fox

This fox eats small prey, such as insects, or fruit. It uses its large ears to detect the movement of insects under the soil before digging them out.

Muscular hips and thighs

Elegant, streamlined body

English setter

These sporting dogs have a keen sense of smell and use it to locate game.

Beagle

Scent hounds, such as this beagle, have been bred for an exceptional sense of smell. Rather than relying on sight, they follow scent trails with remarkable accuracy.

Strong legs and stamina make a great hunter.

EYEWITNESS

Alexandra Horowitz

American cognitive scientist Alexandra Horowitz directs the Dog Cognition Lab at Barnard College in New York, exploring how dogs perceive the world, particularly through their sense of smell. Horowitz is also an author, and her books, including *Inside of a Dog*, have helped readers understand dogs better.

Behavior

Behavior in the dog family is divided into two groups. Solitary hunters—such as foxes and South American wild dogs—live alone, except when mating or raising young. Social hunters—including wolves, jackals, coyotes, African hunting dogs, dholes, and domestic dogs—live more like a family. In these groups, parents usually lead and work together to care for the sick, raise young, and teach survival skills to younger members before they become independent. Wolves lead the pack, not by aggression, but through authority.

EYEWITNESS

Shirin Merchant
With a career spanning more than 20 years, Indian dog trainer Shirin Merchant has worked to promote an understanding of canine behavior and positive dog training methods in the country. She also founded Canines Can Care, an organization that trains dogs for therapy, rescue, and more.

Feeding time

African hunting dogs eat extra meat that is regurgitated for their young or other, weaker pack members.

Body language

Dogs interact with humans and other animals using their posture, ear position, tail movement, and facial expressions.

Solitary hunters

Foxes hunt by themselves, and so do not have the interactive behavior of social hunters. A fox's tail cannot wag as expressively as a wolf's, and its ears are less mobile. But it cowers down if frightened and will stand up tall to look threatening if angry.

Howling instinct

Like its wolf ancestors (left), this husky (below) howls to communicate with others of its kind.

Just good friends

This painting by English artist John Charlton shows dogs of different breeds playing together.

First greetings

Although smaller than the Dalmatian, this Norfolk terrier has a strong personality and is showing confidence.

Puppies

The young of the dog family (Canidae) all look similar when newborn—small, blind, defenseless, and short-haired, with short legs and a little tail. They eat by suckling milk from their mother. The number of young can vary from 1 to 12 or more. After 10 to 14 days, their eyes begin to open, and they can hear shortly after. They soon start eating solid food, which is provided by the mother and, in packs, by other group members. In the wild, young are born in a den; a domestic dog also needs a dark, warm place to give birth.

Four-week-old Great Dane puppies ...

... playfully attacking each other ...

It's playtime

Puppies should be allowed space to play. It helps them learn to interact with other dogs and humans and improve their coordination.

All is well—they're friends again.

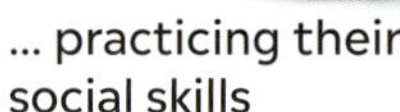

... practicing their social skills

Growing pups

All puppies, including these Great Danes, require a carefully balanced diet of protein, calcium, and vitamins to grow well. They also need training, sleep, affection, and space to exercise their growing limbs.

Nursing

This wolf is suckling her cubs. Soon, their sharp milk teeth will grow, so she will wean the cubs with regurgitated meat.

In 2004, a Neapolitan mastiff gave birth to a record number of 24 puppies in a litter.

Getting carried away

Some canids, such as wolves and domestic dogs, carry their cubs or puppies around by the scruff of the neck or in their mouths.

Learning to behave

The play of these African hunting dog pups, together with lessons from their mother, teaches them social behavior rules, setting them up for adult life as hunters.

A tail of two puppies

This Dalmatian is older than the black Labrador and is the more experienced dog. This difference levels out as they grow.

Four-and-a-half-month-old black Labrador puppy

Dalmatian at six months

Pack **leaders**

Wolf packs are like many human families—the oldest male and female are leaders, and the young do as they are told. Wolves guard their territory and make their presence known by howling. Each pack member knows their role in the familial group. The only wolves to mate are the dominant male and female. After birth, the cubs are suckled for about 10 weeks, then fed with regurgitated meat until they start hunting.

Walking a long road

This group of European wolves is looking for food of any kind, even insects and berries. Wolves can roam across 400 sq miles (1,000 sq km) in packs of up to 20.

Gray wolves

Living in packs of 6–10, gray wolves work together to hunt. But some may temporarily live alone seeking mates or new territory. Wolves have been killed by humans for hundreds of years. Today, they are found in parts of Europe and North America.

Arctic hunter

Arctic wolves work hard to find prey in the harsh Arctic region. A thick, white winter coat camouflages them in snow and ice. In summer, it can be shades of gray, buff, or black. They feed on hares, birds, and, if lucky, deer or musk ox.

Little Red Riding Hood

This story of a very clever wolf tricking a girl has frightened children out of going into forests alone.

Making a meal of it

A pack of wolves chase musk oxen on Ellesmere Island, Canada. Most of the gray wolves in North America live in Canada.

Win or lose

Wolves are quick to defend their territory and often get into fights. Some are killed during these clashes.

Gray wolves run across the snow in Minnesota.

Ethiopian howler

The Ethiopian wolf is in danger of extinction because the high grassland plains where it lives are being taken over by farmers for livestock grazing. Fewer than 450 of these wolves survive in the wild today.

EYEWITNESS

Claudio Sillero-Zubiri

Argentine-born British biologist Professor Claudio Sillero-Zubiri founded the Ethiopian Wolf Conservation Programme to protect the endangered Ethiopian wolf. He also leads global canid conservation through the International Union for Conservation of Nature (IUCN) Canid Specialist Group.

Jackals

Jackals and coyotes come just below wolves in the scale of social hunters (pp. 18–19). There are three species of jackals, all found in Africa: the side-striped jackal and the black-backed jackal live south of the Sahara; the golden jackal is widespread. It is also found in southern Asia and southeastern Europe. Coyotes live only in North America. All form close-knit family groups that forage for food, either scavenging kill left by other carnivores, or killing prey themselves. The whole family helps take care of pups and bring back food.

Golden oldies

This pair of golden jackals will stay together for life. Hunting and breeding as a couple, they patrol their territory, scent-marking it with urine to stop other jackals coming near them.

Coarse, short-haired coat varies from gold to brown, depending on season and region.

Fur saddle

The black-backed jackal has a coat of fine fur with a black or silver saddle.

Fierce face

This Toltec artifact from Mesoamerica shows Quetzalcóatl, the serpent god, wearing a coyote headdress.

White stripe

The side-striped jackal's coat is a mix of colors. A white stripe runs along its side and it has a white-tipped tail.

Every jackal family has a unique wailing call that only its own family members respond to.

The skull is smaller than a wolf's, with a flat forehead and small teeth.

Social coyote

The coyote, also called brush or prairie wolf, is the jackal of North America—a social hunter that lives in pairs and family groups.

Cunning coydog

Wild coyotes may mate with domestic dogs. Their "coydog" pups are not tame, and may kill livestock.

Jackal worship

Anubis, the jackal god, is often shown in ancient Egyptian art.

African-Asian **dogs**

Many wild canids live in Africa and Asia. Social hunters such as jackals live on both continents, and many wolves live in Asia. In Africa, there are hunting dogs and bat-eared foxes, which are not actually foxes. In India and Southeast Asia, Tibetan and Bengal foxes—both solitary hunters—are true fox species (pp. 28–29). "Red dogs" (dholes) and raccoon dogs hunt in groups. Each wild dog or fox has evolved to fill a particular role in its environment, interacting with both prey and other predators.

A pack running together

White tuft at the end of the short, bushy tail acts as a flag.

Unique pattern is tan and gray with white blotches.

African hunting dog

A most sociable dog

The African hunting dog is one of the most social wild canids. Living in large packs on grasslands, it uses an elaborate system of sounds and body movements to communicate, and hunts by day.

Dark gray to black on face mask and muzzle

The tail is up to 13 in (34 cm) long.

Bat-eared fox

Enough teeth

The bat-eared fox has 46–50 teeth (other canids have 42) and feeds mostly on insects.

Two-headed dog

This sacred dog-headed object was made by the Bakongo in the Democratic Republic of Congo.

Indian or Chinese?

The red dog, or dhole, will not interbreed with domestic dogs. The Indian dhole has a lighter coat than the thicker, darker coat of the more northern Chinese dhole.

Rounded ears

Tawny-colored coat

Indian dhole

Long, bushy tail

Dark red coat

Chinese dhole

Raccoon dog

Not to be confused with North American raccoons, the raccoon dog is a short-tailed, chubby canid that lives in Asia. It has been widely bred for its thick coat of gray-black and white fur.

Raccoon dog in winter coat

Raccoon dog in dark summer coat

Red or **gray?**

All foxes are solitary hunters that live on their own—except in mating season. They have long bodies; bushy tails (a "brush"); highly developed senses; and large, erect ears. Their usual prey are rodents and rabbits. The red fox is very common, and easily adapts to different environments. There are ten other species in the fox group, or genus *Vulpes*. The gray fox of North and Central America belongs to the genus *Urocyon* and can climb trees.

Gray coat
The gray fox is found in the US, Central America, and northern South America.

Nose and sides of muzzle are black.

Tip of the tail may be blackish, or grey like the coat.

Getting to the top
The gray fox climbs trees to look for prey, which can be rabbits, insects, or dead animals. It is gray like salt and pepper, and has reddish underparts.

Waiting for lunch
Fox cubs stay with their mother for months before they find their own territories.

On the hunt

In the past, foxes were sometimes considered pests because they killed chickens and game birds. Today, fox hunting is a countryside sport for the rich in some countries. However, many people believe it to be cruel.

Furry beautiful

Foxes have beautiful pelts that keep them warm in winter. People have made clothes from red fox pelts for thousands of years. Captive foxes have also been bred for furs to be used in fashion. In modern times, this is unacceptable to many.

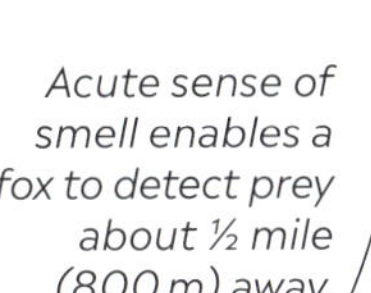

Acute sense of smell enables a fox to detect prey about ½ mile (800 m) away.

Coat can range in color from grayish- and rust-red to a flame red.

A red fox can hear a rodent moving underground miles away.

White-tipped tail

Red fox?

This black (melanistic) form of the red fox was painted by American artist John James Audubon. There are many shades of red fox including silver!

Streetwise

In some cities, foxes are common. They kill rats, scavenge in trash cans, and even learn road sense.

Hot and cold **foxes**

A few foxes lead harsh lives in the coldest and hottest lands. The Arctic fox lives in the icy northern regions of Europe, Asia, Alaska, and Canada. It has short ears to stop heat loss, dense fur to keep warm, and can cover vast distances in search of food. Other foxes live in deserts where there is little food, so they too hunt and scavenge across huge areas. Desert foxes have very large ears to stay cool and small bodies that need little food; they shelter in dens during the day.

EYEWITNESS

Toralf Mjøen

For more than 15 years Toralf Mjøen has worked as a caretaker at the Arctic Fox Captive Breeding Station in Norway. He has been breeding Arctic foxes in captivity and releasing them into the wild to prevent their extinction. Since the onset of the program, their population has increased from 40 to around 550.

Arctic fox cub's summer coat

Adult Arctic foxes in pale winter coat

Seasonal colors

In the high Arctic, where there is usually snow, the Arctic fox has a white, or polar, winter coat (right). In summer, it will have a brown-and-white coat (above). Molting occurs in spring and fall.

Kit fox

This desert fox lives in the southwestern US and Mexico. It is preyed on by coyotes, and is threatened by humans, too.

Sand fox

This desert fox from North Africa and the Arabian Desert looks similar to a fennec fox but is larger in size. It hides from the heat underground during the day and hunts at night.

Fennec fox

The world's smallest fox is the fennec fox. It lives in the Sahara in Africa, and in the parched deserts of Arabia, where food is always scarce.

Foxy **zorros**

South American wild canids are often called foxes, or zorros (Spanish for foxes), but they are not true foxes. They are solitary hunters of small animals, but will eat anything they find. There are four groups, or genera, of fox-like dogs: the maned wolf; the short-legged bush dog; the crab-eating fox; and six members of the *Lycalopex* genus, including the culpeo, chilla, and Azara zorros.

Azara's fox

Found in the Pampas grasslands of South America, this gray-bodied, red-headed zorro has a very long, bushy tail.

Patagonian fox

Also known as chilla, the Patagonian fox lives in the southern part of South America. Like many canids in the genus *Lycalopex*, it is not at all timid.

Culpeo

This zorro lives on slopes and plateaus along the Andes mountain range.

Small ears

Broad face

Bush dog

Like other South American members of the dog family, the bush dog is not a true dog or fox, but belongs in a group on its own—the genus *Speothos*. It is found in open country near water in tropical South America.

Maned wolves are solitary animals but they mate for life, and help raise their cubs when young.

The maned wolf has a short tail compared to its legs and body.

Crab-eating fox

This zorro feasts on crabs during the wet season in the forests of northeastern South America.

Magnificent mane

Neither fox nor wolf, the maned wolf belongs to the genus *Chrysocyon*. It stands very tall, with legs longer than its body and its tail ending well above ground. It lives in grasslands in southern Brazil and pounces on small animals.

Dear **dogs**

Domestic dogs are descended from an extinct population of gray wolves. Humans probably first domesticated wolves during the last Ice Age (100,000–25,000 years ago). The people of ancient Egypt and western Asia were the first to breed distinctive kinds of dogs. By Roman times, most of the dog shapes and sizes that we know today already existed. This is known from skeletal remains, and from works of art that portray the animals in detail. In the ancient world, dogs were kept as hunting, herding, and guard dogs, as well as for sport and companionship.

Jackal figurine

The jackal has always lived close to humans, but it is not an ancestor of the domestic dog.

Statue of Anubis, the ancient Egyptian jackal god

Persian plaque

This stylized half-dog, half-bird, or "senmurv" was made in silver during the Sasanian Dynasty (c. 7th century BCE).

This plaque was found in India.

Hound-shaped handle

Flagon

A Celtic bronze drinking vessel (c. 400 BCE) shows two hounds chasing a duck swimming up the spout.

Huntsmen

Assyrian huntsmen with mastiff-like hounds were carved on a palace wall in Nineveh, Iraq, in 645–635 BCE.

Eastern worship

In East Asia, dogs are often included in Buddhist religious worship. This lionlike dog statue stands guard in a temple in Thailand.

The statue holding a cub indicates that this guardian dog is female.

Greek urn

This vase, found in southern Italy, is of Greek design (c. 380–360 BCE). The girl is dangling a tortoise to tease her pet dog.

Guard dog

Mosaics with dogs and the words *cave canem* ("beware of the dog") were popular in Rome.

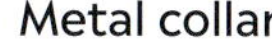

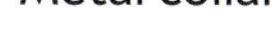

Dog collars

Ever since Egyptian times, dogs in paintings and sculptures have been shown wearing collars. This historical dog collar is from England.

Metal collar

Marble hounds

The ancient Romans used greyhounds and bloodhounds for hunting, and large mastiffs as fighting and war dogs.

Roman marble of two hounds

Woman and dog

This is the skeleton of a woman, buried with her hand on her dog. The 12,000-year-old remains, found in the southern Levant, are one of the earliest examples of a domestic dog.

Dog rose

The ancient Greeks used the dog rose plant to treat people bitten by rabid dogs. However, it is not effective.

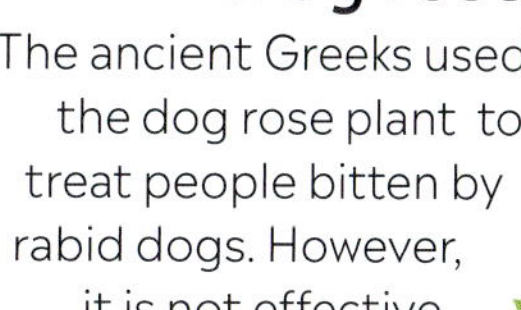

Feral **dogs**

The first dogs were domesticated more than 14,000 years ago. Some of them later reverted to a wild lifestyle and are known as "feral" dogs. Feral dogs may scavenge near human settlements, but live and breed independently. In some regions, dogs live entirely without human contact, such as the dingo of Australia, which arrived on the continent around 8,300 years ago. Similar populations exist in parts of Asia and Africa. These dogs typically inhabit the outskirts of villages, surviving by foraging in trash and fending for themselves.

Ancient breed

A pottery vessel from the Colima, Mexico (300–900 CE), depicts a hairless, fattened techichi.

An Indian pariah dog's skull from 2500 BCE was unearthed in the ruins of the Indus Valley civilization.

Indie dog

Pariah dogs have been living wild in India for thousands of years. Some look very like the dingoes of Australia. This pack has chosen to keep cool on a sandy beach in Goa, India.

A pointy snout and ears sit on a wedge-shaped head.

The reddish-brown coat is short and dense.

Scavenging for food

The feral dogs of Egypt are called Baladi, which means "local." With a population that runs into millions, these strays try and find scraps of food left by tourists.

Dominant dingo

These young dingoes are practicing their social skills.

The Australian dog

Dingoes are very successful at living in the wild. But we now know they were originally domestic dogs, taken to Australia by First Nations people 4,000 years ago. They may be the only purebred descendants of prehistoric domestic dogs in the world.

Mother and babies

Dingoes mate once a year and raise their pups as social hunters.

Breeding **dogs**

Many dog breeds are hundreds of years old, but a new one can be developed by crossing two or more different breeds. It is also possible to reconstitute (remake) an extinct breed, such as the Irish wolfhound, which died out 100 years ago and was bred as a new line from Great Danes, deerhounds, and mastiffs. Before the first dog show in England, in 1859, dogs of a single breed varied in size, shape, and color. Today, showing standards mean dogs of one breed look very much alike, and can be at risk from similar inherited ailments.

Lurcher, made for speed

Turned-up corners of the mouth create a "smile."

Mighty muscles

The Staffordshire bull terrier was developed as a fighting dog, by crossing the bull terrier, bulldog, and Old English terrier. Today, they are bred to be sweet-natured, loyal pets, especially calm and patient around young children.

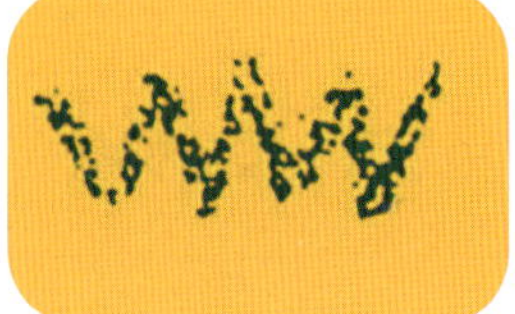

Dog

Bad dog

Secret symbols

American migrant workers used signs to say if there was a dog or bad dog on a property.

Lurcher

Successful cross

Originally a cross between a speedy greyhound with great sight and a robust terrier, the lurcher was used by poachers. Today, many different breeds are crossed to create lurchers, so it's considered a "type" rather than a breed.

Danish-Swedish farmdog

Breed or not?

The Danish-Swedish farmdog (left) was recognized as a breed by the Swedish Kennel Club in 1987, but by the American Kennel Club much later in 2025. Kennel Clubs across countries have different rules for officially recognizing a dog breed.

EYEWITNESS

Alain Thomas

Welsh animal welfare advocate Alain Thomas cofounded Greyhound Rescue Wales in 1993. He has dedicated decades to rescuing and rehoming abandoned greyhounds and lurchers, promoting care for former working dogs.

Jack Russell terriers

The rough and the smooth

First bred in the 1800s by Englishman Jack Russell, these small dogs were produced by several now-extinct breeds and varied in appearance. Their coats can be short and smooth, long and rough-haired, or both. In the US, this breed is split into two—the Parson Russell, and the Russell terrier.

Streamlined body and short-haired coat

Long, slim legs

During World War II, lurchers were used as guard dogs and messengers.

Hunting **dogs**

Hunting in India

The Mughal emperors of India, such as Akbar (1542–1605), hunted antelope with Saluki-type hounds.

Dogs were used in hunting wild animals for centuries. In medieval times, rulers and feudal lords of Europe and Asia hunted from horseback with dogs. The laws of hunting were very complicated, and certain animals were preserved for the nobility to hunt. Special breeds of scent and sight hounds (pp. 14–17) were used during these hunts. The most valuable dogs were the now extinct buckhounds, used for hunting fallow deer.

Hunt depicted in Bening's *Book of Hours* (16th century)

Medieval hunting dogs

In Europe, medieval huntsmen usually had 12 running hounds and a lyme-hound (scent hound), which frightened game out of its hiding place.

Hunting horn

Blowing the horn with a series of long and short notes was a key part of medieval hunting rituals.

The Savernake Horn, made of ivory in 12th-century England

Running with the pack

The bold, strong, intelligent beagle has ancient origins. Over time, it went through many changes before looking like the dogs in this 19th-century painting by Alfred Duke.

Gamekeeping

Since medieval times, the job of a gamekeeper, like the one shown here with his dogs, has included protecting game from poachers.

Hunting in Benin

This brass plaque, made by an artist in the Kingdom of Benin in the 16th century, shows a Portuguese soldier with his hunting dog.

Swimming dog

Most dogs enjoy a swim, but retrievers are specially bred to bring back birds that have been shot and fallen into the water. They have a "soft mouth," which means they can carry a dead bird without biting into it. Their fur has a very water-resistant undercoat.

Golden retriever

Webbed feet help retrievers swim easily.

Herding **dogs**

Fluffy tail
Old English sheepdogs used to have their tails docked, but this is now banned in many countries.

The use of dogs to protect and herd livestock dates from around 1000 BCE when farmers began to keep large numbers of animals. In ancient Rome, the writer Columella noted that shepherds preferred white sheepdogs so they would not mistake them for a wolf killing their animals.

Border collie

Originally from the border of England and Scotland, the border collie is one of the world's finest sheepdogs.

Rough collie

This traditional sheepdog of the Scottish lowlands is probably so-called from a "colley" (local black sheep). Today, it is a popular show breed and companion.

Blue heeler

Now called the Australian cattle dog, this breed of strong working dog rounds up cattle by nipping at their heels.

Short and straight coat

Belgian shepherd

Slightly smaller than a German shepherd, the Belgian shepherd has four varieties, with differences in coat types, from long to short, or smooth to wiry. Their colors can range from fawn to red, gray, or black.

A goatherd and his dog

This Tajik goatherd and his thick-coated Central Asian shepherd dog are prepared for winter as they herd goats in the Pamir mountains in Tajikistan.

Herding dogs can understand even small hand signals.

Small sheltie

Domestic animals on the Shetland Isles, UK, tend to be very small to better survive tough conditions. The Shetland sheepdog, or sheltie, is a successful product of breeding for small size—it is up to 15 in (40 cm) high at its shoulders.

Helpers

Dogs have been indispensable helpers throughout history, to herd other animals, for companionship, and as guardians of the home and business premises—although to shut a dog in an enclosed space on its own goes against the dog's social behavioral patterns and is cruel. Certain breeds have the genetic potential for aggression, but nearly all dogs have to be specially trained to be aggressive to strangers and not to their handlers. Today, dogs also help the sick, disabled, and lonely.

Dogs of war

Dogs' loyalty to people means they can be trained for dangerous missions in wars and conflict zones.

Sturdy jaw—with the lower jaw projecting above the upper one

Powerful forequarters are inherited from the bulldog.

Rescue dogs

Dogs bred at the monastery of the Great Saint Bernard Pass in Switzerland were trained to rescue people stuck in the snowy mountains. With their keen sense of smell, St. Bernard dogs found people buried in snow, could dig and reach them, and also kept them warm until they were rescued.

Boxer

Dew claws on forelegs

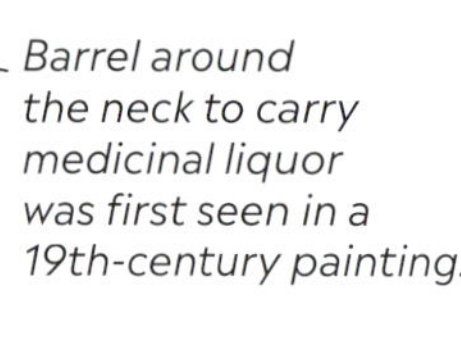

Barrel around the neck to carry medicinal liquor was first seen in a 19th-century painting.

Bernese mountain dog

The dogs known as Swiss mountain dogs until the 1900s today have four breeds: Bernese (p. 56), Appenzell, Entlebucher, and Greater Swiss. They are good rescue dogs.

Fierce protector

Bred in Germany in the 19th century, the Doberman pinscher is sleek and muscular, loyal, and highly intelligent. It is a born guard dog, but can be an affectionate companion if trained and socialized that way.

Good company

Boxers and German shepherds are guard dogs, first bred in Germany. The boxer is of mastiff origin crossed with the bulldog, and the German shepherd is a herding dog. Both are good companions if reared correctly, but need plenty of space and exercise.

A German shepherd needs to repeat a task just five times to learn it.

Continued on next page

Continued from previous page

Seeing eye dogs

Specially trained to guide blind people, seeing eye dogs help their humans navigate safely around obstacles, and live more independently. Their bond is built on trust and teamwork.

Guide dogs know when to disobey commands and act in the best interest of their human.

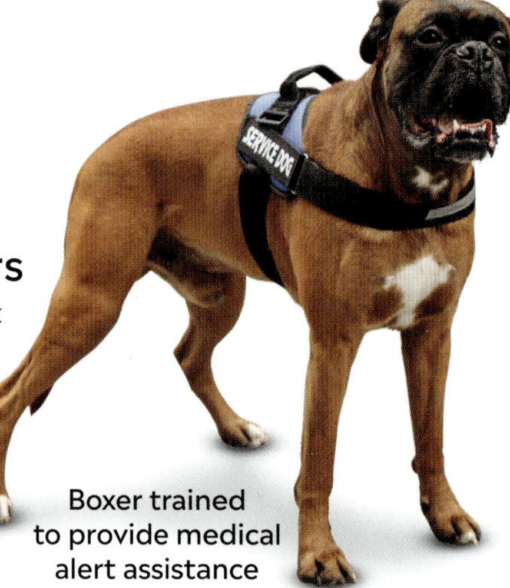

Boxer trained to provide medical alert assistance

Medical alert helpers

Some lifesaving dogs can detect subtle changes in their owner's scent or behavior. They can alert their humans about impending seizures, diabetic crashes, or other medical emergencies—often before symptoms even appear.

EYEWITNESS

Sunday Agbonika

Nigerian veterinarian and dog trainer Dr. Sunday Agbonika pioneered animal-assisted services for neurodivergent children in Nigeria. He founded the Dogalov HumAn Support Initiative, introducing therapy dogs that can provide support and develop these children's social skills.

Social signal dogs

Therapy dogs can help autistic children feel calmer and better understood. They provide emotional support, encourage communication, and ease social situations through companionship and nonverbal connection.

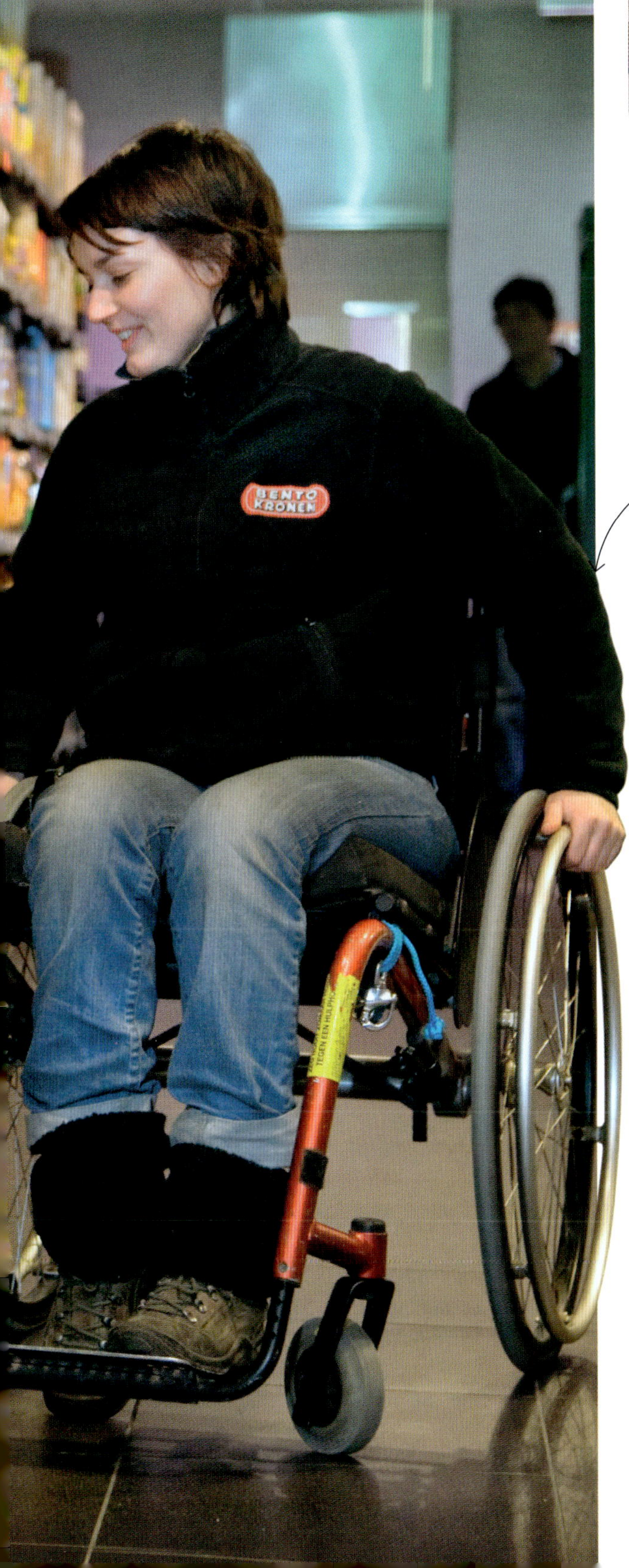

Mobility assistance dogs

People with physical disabilities can get help from mobility assistance dogs in everyday tasks. These dogs can open doors, retrieve dropped items, and even help with shopping. Large breeds, such as Labradors and golden retrievers, are preferred because they are strong enough to assist their handlers.

A wheelchair-bound woman shops with her Labrador mobility assistance dog.

Veteran service dogs

Trained to support veterans with post-traumatic stress disorder (PTSD), veteran service dogs can help reduce anxiety in soldiers. These service dogs can recognize PTSD symptoms and calm the veterans by doing specific tasks such as nudging or applying pressure.

Pet goldendoodle

Beloved pets

Dogs bring love, companionship, and joy to families. They teach empathy, support emotional well-being, promote an active lifestyle, and help children grow in confidence and responsibility.

Hounds

When dogs were separated into groups, hounds were one of the most distinctive. At a later stage, hounds were split into lightly built, very fast sight hounds used in the hunt to chase prey, and heavily built scent hounds used to sniff out prey. Hounds vary in size more than any other dog group. The Irish wolfhound is the tallest dog; the dachshund, one of the smallest. Many breeds are still used for hunting; others are house dogs and companions.

Faithful pets

Hounds make loyal pets and have long been described as such in stories. According to a Welsh legend, Prince Llywelyn killed his deerhound Gelert, thinking the dog had killed his child. But then he found the baby safe, and nearby a dead wolf, killed by his faithful dog.

Afghan hound

This ancient breed of long-haired hound came from Afghanistan, where the royal family used it for hunting. A popular show dog, it still has hunting and racing instincts.

Bloodhound

Excellent trackers, bloodhounds were originally bred to find prey for hunters. They are now used in some countries to track missing people and criminals.

Medieval hunter

The foxhound does not make a good house dog because for centuries it has been bred only for hunting and living in a pack.

Irish wolfhound

Used in Ireland for hunting in medieval times, and re-created in the late 1800s, this breed looks like a rough-haired greyhound. It is the tallest dog in the world, with a shoulder height of 3 ft (94 cm).

Bundle of energy

The beagle was originally bred to track hares in Britain and France. It is still used for hunting, but can be a great family dog, as long as it gets lots of exercise.

Long, muscular hind legs help chase prey over great distances.

Hunting tapestry

This detail is from a Flemish tapestry woven in the early 1400s. It shows a medieval hunting scene with richly dressed ladies and noblemen, their hounds, and boar prey.

Irish wolfhound

"Weiner" dog

Dachshund means "badger dog" in German, because they were originally used to dig out badgers from their dens. "Hund" was translated as "hound," and so the dogs were classed in that group.

The dachshund can be short-haired, long-haired, or, as here, wire-haired.

Sporting **dogs**

Spaniels, setters, pointers, and retrievers are all "sporting dogs" (North America), or "gun dogs" (Britain). They are not usually aggressive, and are today mostly used in the shooting of game birds. They are trained to "point" and "set"—scent the air for birds, then crouch still and silent to alert the hunters. They must have soft mouths to retrieve prey and not damage it. Sporting dogs respond well to training, and so are also bred as house dogs and companions.

Silky coat

Red-haired beauty

The Irish, or red, setter has a gentle nature, but is high strung and headstrong—not ideal for a sporting dog.

Long, silky coat protects against cold weather in open areas.

Powerful haunches aid the dog in running quickly.

A real charmer

The American cocker spaniel got its name from flushing out woodcock birds.

Muscular, strong-boned legs help the cocker to be an excellent bird dog.

Duck-hunters

Spaniels have been bred for centuries as water dogs. In this painting are a Chesapeake Bay retriever, an Irish water spaniel, and a curly coated retriever.

German short-haired pointer

Large ears help capture and hold scented prey.

Getting the point

Pointers are trained to "point" at game with their noses.

Old Danish pointer

When pointers sense prey, they stop with their head leaning toward the smell.

Retrievers

Dogs such as this golden retriever are trained to retrieve game that has been shot.

Multi-talented

Despite its name, the German short-haired pointer is also an excellent retriever, both on land and in water.

Terriers

Terriers are "earth dogs"—*terra* means "earth" in Latin. They are great diggers and will happily go down holes after badgers, foxes, rabbits, or rats. Terriers have an ancient history as small sporting and hunting dogs. Different types of terrier have been bred in many regions of Britain, but a few other countries have also developed new breeds, such as the Australian terrier.

EYEWITNESS

Edwin Hautenville Richardson

Recognizing how clever terriers were, British Army officer Edwin Richardson trained Airedale terriers during World War I (1914–1918) for military tasks in the war zone, including message delivery and finding wounded men. He founded the British War Dog School for their training in 1917.

Shaggy dog story

Early British immigrants to Australia took their dogs. By the early 1900s, the Australian terrier had been developed from a range of terriers.

Long, strong jaws help the Australian terrier catch rats, rabbits, and even snakes.

Scottie dog

The modern Scottish terrier is descended from working terriers of the Scottish Highlands.

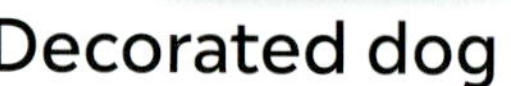

Decorated dog

Dogs are popular mascots with army regiments, such as this brave war hero, "Drummer"—mascot of the Northumberland Fusiliers.

The ears are slightly rounded at the tip.

Norfolk terrier

Like a lamb

All sorts of breeds contributed to the distinctive features of the Bedlington terrier.

Bedlington terrier

The tip of the Airedale's small, V-shaped ear falls forward to its eye.

Tail is set well up, and carried erect, not curved forwards.

Stiff, wiry coat lying close to the body needs careful grooming.

Devoted pet

When his master died in Edinburgh, Scotland, a Skye terrier, Bobby, lay on the grave until his own death 14 years later. A monument erected in his name is a popular tourist destination today.

With excellent balance, a wire-haired fox terrier is ready for action.

The giant Airedale terrier

The largest of all terriers was developed in the mid-1800s by cross-breeding the black-and-tan terrier with the large, strong otterhound.

Fox terrier

In the late 1800s, this was England's most popular breed; today, it is the smaller Jack Russell. Fox terriers can be wire- or smooth-haired.

Playful terrier

This new breed, descended from terriers bred in East Anglia, England, has a low-slung body, short legs, and a wiry coat. It was given the name of Norfolk in 1965.

Non-sporting **dogs**

Mainly classified as non-sporting dogs in the US, the UK's "utility" group includes breeds that haven't been allotted into the other groups (hounds, sporting dogs, herding dogs, terriers, working dogs, and toy dogs). "Special dogs" might be a more apt name to cover their many, varied characteristics, as they include the more interesting, unusual dogs. For some, their history goes back many centuries, and most of this group have been bred for a particular purpose.

A giant schnauzer stands up to 2 ft (65 cm) at the shoulder.

Muzzle is adorned by a massive mustache.

A flat face can cause medical issues including breathing distress, dental problems, and skin conditions.

Legs are set wide apart, allowing the dog to stand its ground.

French bulldog

Bat-eared bulldog

Bulldogs were once bred for baiting animals including bulls, a cruel sport that is now banned. Today, bulldogs are smaller and calmer, but are still tough and make good guard dogs.

The tongue of the chow chow is always blue-black.

Curled tail and very thick fur

Chinese chow

The chow chow breed was developed from two dogs of feral origin from northern China that were introduced into England in the 1780s.

Schnauzers

So-called from *Schnauze*, meaning "muzzle" in German, and bred for herding sheep in southern Germany, these energetic dogs make good family pets today. They come in three sizes: miniature, standard, and giant. In the US, they are grouped under working dogs.

New breed

The Boston terrier is one of the few breeds to have been developed in the US.

Ears are rounded at the tip.

The dense, double coat is coarse and weather-resistant.

Coat is always white with black or brown (liver) spots.

Legs are long and built for speed and endurance.

Dalmatian

Spotted dog

Dalmatians were first taken to England in the 18th century, where these aristocratic-looking dogs were used as coach dogs.

Pretty as a picture

Poodles were bred as sporting dogs, but their intelligence and attractiveness soon led to their becoming house dogs. This painting shows an early 18th century form of the pet.

Working **dogs**

Around 12,000 years ago, some wolf species were tamed and later bred to be the first domestic dogs, as companions to human hunters. Dogs have worked with people ever since. Indigenous North American peoples used dogs to pull a sled and in bison hunts. In Europe, sled dogs were used for reindeer herding and polar expeditions.

Panting makes dogs lose heat through their tongue and cool down after running.

Swimming champ

The Newfoundland dog is an excellent swimmer and is used for rescues. It may come from Pyrenean mountain rescue dogs taken to Newfoundland, Canada, by Spanish fishermen.

Agile Aussie

Australian kelpies round up sheep that have strayed from the main flock. They can travel up to 40 miles (64 km) in a day.

Thick, moderately long coat

Swiss blanket

The Bernese mountain dog is one of many mastiff-type dogs used for rescues, guarding, and protecting people in mountains. By staying next to a person, it can keep them warm during rescues, and it can use its nose to find the way through thick snow.

Thick ruff of fur around neck, and stocky shape keep as much warmth inside the husky's body as possible.

The working dog's harness is designed to give it the greatest pulling power.

Siberian husky

The tail trails when the dog is at rest, but curves up during a run.

Ready for work

The Siberian husky and Alaskan malamute are the only pure breeds of husky. But the name is used in North America for all dogs of the spitz type, used for pulling sleds and hunting.

A malamute is part of the
coat of arms
for Canada's Yukon territory.

On a break

Huskies are an integral part of the culture of the Arctic region, and are used regularly as sled dogs to move people and goods across the snowy landscape. These huskies (left) are taking a break before carrying on with their journey.

Deep and powerful chest

When is a Dane not a Dane?

The Great Dane was developed in Germany for guarding castles.

Toy dogs

This category includes all the smallest show breeds, mostly with a height of less than 12 in (30.5 cm). These small dogs are usually friendly and show their feelings with their posture and tail. The Romans were probably the first to breed miniature dogs. Tiny dogs have been bred since ancient times in China and Japan, too. In Europe, toy spaniels became the favorite companions of the aristocracy in the Middle Ages.

Chinese lion dog figurine

Chinese lion dog

Another name for the Pekingese is "lion dog." Legend says that they were bred to represent the lion spirit of the Buddha.

Toy terrier terror

The Australian silky terrier can kill a rat, rabbit, or even snake in seconds. It looks like a Yorkshire terrier, but apparently originated by cross-breeding in Australia.

Fine, long, silky-textured coat

Dog's dinner

This 19th-century French painting, *Caninemania*, shows the family pet treated as a dinner guest.

Large, broad head with very flat profile and a snub nose

Pekingese pair

Like other flat-faced dog breeds such as pugs and bulldogs, the Pekingese can suffer discomfort and many illnesses, such as breathing troubles, eye disorders, and skin conditions.

Pomeranian

A miniature spitz, the Pomeranian has the stocky body, pricked ears, ruff of fur, and curled tail that is typical of spitz dogs.

King Charles spaniel

Royal favorite

Probably originating in China or Japan, this good-tempered dog was named due to English king Charles II's fondness for it.

Popular pinscher

This energetic German breed was originally used to control vermin. They have great hearing and make good, if small, guard dogs.

Tail of the Bichon is always curled over its back.

Bichon frise

Looking like a small poodle, this is a lively and intelligent little dog. *Frisé*—French for "curly"—is a good description of the breed. This breed is classified as a non-sporting dog and not a toy dog in the US.

White coat has a soft, woolly underfur covered by loosely curled, silky hairs.

Toy dogs can weigh less than 10 lb (4.5 kg).

Cross-bred **dogs**

The development of dog breeds spans more than 5,000 years. Today, however, most dogs are still mongrels—cross-bred dogs that have interbred, and have inherited a mix of traits from many breeds. In contrast, purebred dogs come from the same breed and have been selectively bred by humans to maintain specific traits. It is often claimed that cross-bred dogs are more intelligent than purebreds, but it is more accurate to say that their behavior can vary widely, as they inherit a broader combination of characteristics from different breeds.

All 400 breeds of dog can interbreed because they are the same species.

Giant leap for dogkind

These pictures show the movements of a cross-bred dog that jumps over an obstacle. The tail is important for keeping balance.

Tail arched upward helps the dog retain its balance.

Strong, well-muscled legs help the dog jump high off the ground.

Stance for takeoff

"His master's voice"

This painting, of a cross-breed called Nipper, was bought by a gramophone company. The picture and slogan were trademarked in 1910 and are still in use.

Good dog!

Training a dog to establish good behavior patterns can be a long and arduous process.

Strong, well-proportioned legs

Terra-cotta dog

This small figure was made of terra-cotta in Greece in 500 BCE. It shows a dog with an alert tail.

Dog's best friend

This 19th-century painting shows a man sharing his food with a large group of mongrels.

Motley crew

Not bred for extreme tasks, cross-bred dogs such as these are often tougher, better-tempered, less disease-prone, and more adaptable than purebreds.

Dog care

Black miniature poodle

1 Ready and waiting for a grooming session

A dog can live longer than 17 years. It needs a good home, which provides shelter, comfort, and care. Dogs need training, exercise, and guidance but should still be allowed to behave naturally. They need to be fed a suitable diet and always have fresh water available. They should be registered with a vet and receive checkups and any treatment, if required. Dogs also need friends and should not be left alone for long periods. Many people now insure their dogs.

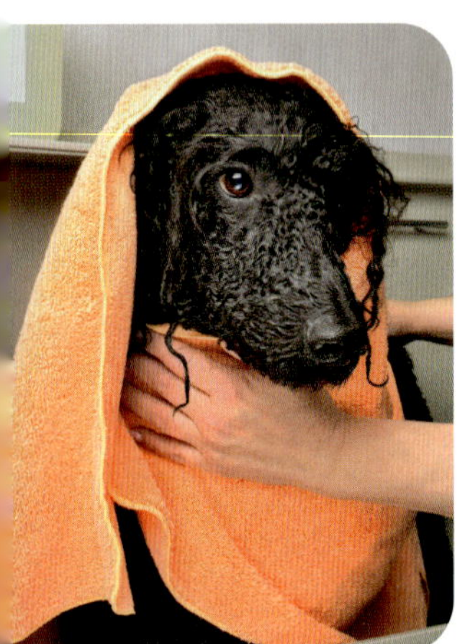

2 Bath time

3 Combing out the knots

4 Trimming the face

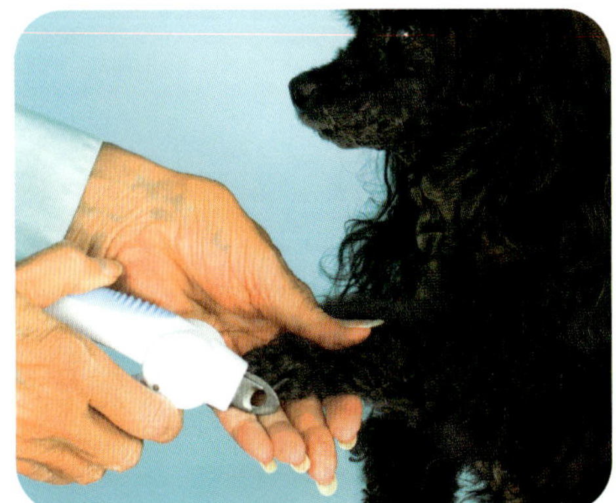

5 Clipping the nails

6 Trimming the jagged edges

Stay warm

Poodles were bred to retrieve game from water and have curly, waterproof hair. This distinct haircut with fluffy legs and joints began as a way to keep them warm in the cold water.

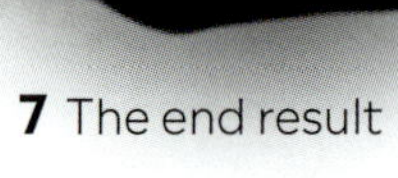

7 The end result

Essential aids

Caring for a dog takes effort and dedicated tools that can be used to keep them fed and clean. Specific foods, everyday grooming tools, and toys are just some of them.

Dish of meat and gravy

Dish of dry kibbles

Brush and comb

Assortment of dog treats

Bowl of water

Collar

Lead

Favorite toys

And so to bed

In the same way that a wild wolf has its own den, every domestic dog needs its own bed. This can be a basket, a bean bag, or a special chair.

EYEWITNESS

Ittikorn Thepmani

A passionate canine advocate, Thai businessman Ittikorn Thepmani cofounded Orgafeed, a company that makes pet food from insects such as crickets and black soldier fly larvae, among others. Apart from being nutritious, insect protein may help pets with food allergies. It is also more environmentally-friendly, taking fewer resources to make than food based on livestock farming.

Did you **know?**

A female suckling her young

AMAZING FACTS

- Dogs can smell and hear better than they can see. Dogs see things first by movement, second by brightness, and third by shape.
- Rhodesian ridgebacks have a visible ridge of forward-growing hairs running along their back.
- A dog's sense of smell is massively better than ours. Dogs can detect which direction a smell comes from. They can detect disease in humans, find missing people, and they are even being used to find bed bugs!
- Hair from some dogs, such as the Samoyed, can be spun into thread and woven into clothes.

Basenji

- The basenji, an African dog from the Congo region, is the only dog breed not able to bark.
- Dogs can hear high-pitched sounds that humans are not aware of, can hear from a great distance, and can figure out the direction of a faint sound.

A Newfoundland dog swimming

- Newfoundland dogs are good swimmers. Like many breeds, they have webbing between their toes, helping them paddle through water.
- Long-faced dogs have eyes on the sides of their head, and so have a wider field of vision. Short-faced dogs tend to have forward-facing eyes, and so are good at judging distances.
- A puppy is deaf for three weeks, until its ear canals open up.
- Bulldogs were originally bred to bait and fight bulls and bears.
- Dogs have about 10 vocal sounds; cats, about 20. Dogs communicate a lot by body language—puppies know signals before words.
- Almost one in three families in France and the US owns a dog. In Germany and Switzerland, there is only one dog for every 10 households.
- Big dogs tend to have larger litters than small dogs, but small dogs usually live longer.
- On average there are 320 bones in a dog's skeleton, depending on the length of the dog's tail.
- The first dog in space was called Laika. In 1957, Russian scientists sent the dog in a satellite.
- The saluki, which has been around since 329 BCE, is the world's oldest dog breed.
- Dogs eat quickly and can regurgitate food easily. This is useful for wolves, who can travel back to their dens to regurgitate for pups, and for dogs to get rid of bad food.
- Most puppies have 28 temporary teeth, which they begin to lose at about 12 weeks. They have usually grown their 42 permanent teeth by the time they are six months old.
- Unlike cats, dogs cannot retract (pull in) their claws.
- Bloodhounds have an amazing sense of smell. They can follow scent trails that are four days old.

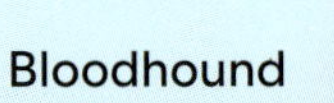

Bloodhound

QUESTIONS AND ANSWERS

Why do the police use dogs?

Because of the dogs' excellent sense of smell. "Sniffer" dogs help the police track down escaped prisoners, and find illegal drugs.

Why do dogs chase their tail?

A puppy instinctively chases its tail, perhaps because it resembles moving prey. If an adult dog chases its tail, it is because of boredom or to get attention from the owner.

Which dogs are the cleverest?

Most sheepdog and sporting dog breeds are intelligent and easy to train. Some smaller breeds are good at performing tricks.

How should you approach a strange dog?

To get close to an unfamiliar dog, always let the dog approach you and let them sniff you. Do not make sudden movements or stare into its eyes, which might feel like a threat. Do not run—that might encourage it to chase you.

Why do dogs pant?

Unlike people, dogs cannot cool themselves by perspiring. They have sweat glands only in their feet. But panting helps a dog stay cool, and saliva evaporating from the tongue and mouth helps reduce its body heat.

Why do dogs eat grass?

Experts believe this can be for a variety of reasons—to aid digestion, to make themselves vomit if they have an upset stomach, or even just because they like the taste.

What is a dorgi?

When a dachshund and a corgi mate, their offspring are called dorgis.

Why do dogs' eyes glow in the dark?

A layer of cells, called the tapetum lucidum, at the back of each eye of a dog reflects light, making it possible for it to see in dim light. When a bright light strikes a dog's eyes, it is reflected, making the eyes appear to glow.

Can dogs see in color?

A dog's color vision is limited to gray, yellow, and blue. The colors green, red, and orange look the same to dogs.

Border collies often herd sheep.

A dog searching a car for drugs

RECORD BREAKERS

The oldest dog
An Australian cattle dog named Bluey lived to be 29 years and 5 months old.

The heaviest and longest dog
An Old English mastiff named Zorba holds the record as the heaviest and longest dog. In 1989, it weighed 342 lb (155 kg) and was 8 ft 3 in (2.5 m) long.

The smallest and tallest breeds
The smallest breed of dog is the chihuahua. Dogs from a number of breeds can be 36 in (90 cm) at the shoulder, and they are classed as the tallest breeds—the Great Dane, Irish wolfhound, St. Bernard, English mastiff, borzoi, and Anatolian karabash.

Great Dane

Identifying **dogs**

Dogs come in different shapes and sizes. The American Kennel Club recognizes 200 breeds, and divides them into seven groups, according to the dog's role.

Dalmatian

Non-sporting dogs

This group contains many dog breeds that haven't been allotted into one of the other groups (hounds, sporting, herding, terriers, working, and toy dogs). The Dalmatian was once used for trotting alongside carriages to deter attackers.

Bloodhounds

Hounds

People have long bred dogs to catch other animals. Some very fast hounds are "sight" hounds, which means that they chase things they can see. Other hounds have great stamina and pursue by scent.

Sporting dogs

These friendly and intelligent dogs require lots of exercise. The group includes pointers, setters, retrievers, and spaniels like this English springer spaniel. Some are still used as hunting dogs.

COAT TYPES

Short-haired dogs have a smooth coat. Most long-haired breeds have a thick undercoat with a longer coat on top. Wire-haired dogs have a short undercoat with longer, wiry hairs on top. A few breeds have a corded, felt-like coat.

Long-haired Old English sheepdog

Wire-haired schnauzer

Short-haired Entlebucher mountain dog

Hungarian puli

HEAD SHAPES

Long-headed dogs have a long, often tapering nose. Round-headed breeds have a short nose. Square-headed dogs have a step between the muzzle and the forehead. It is known as the "stop."

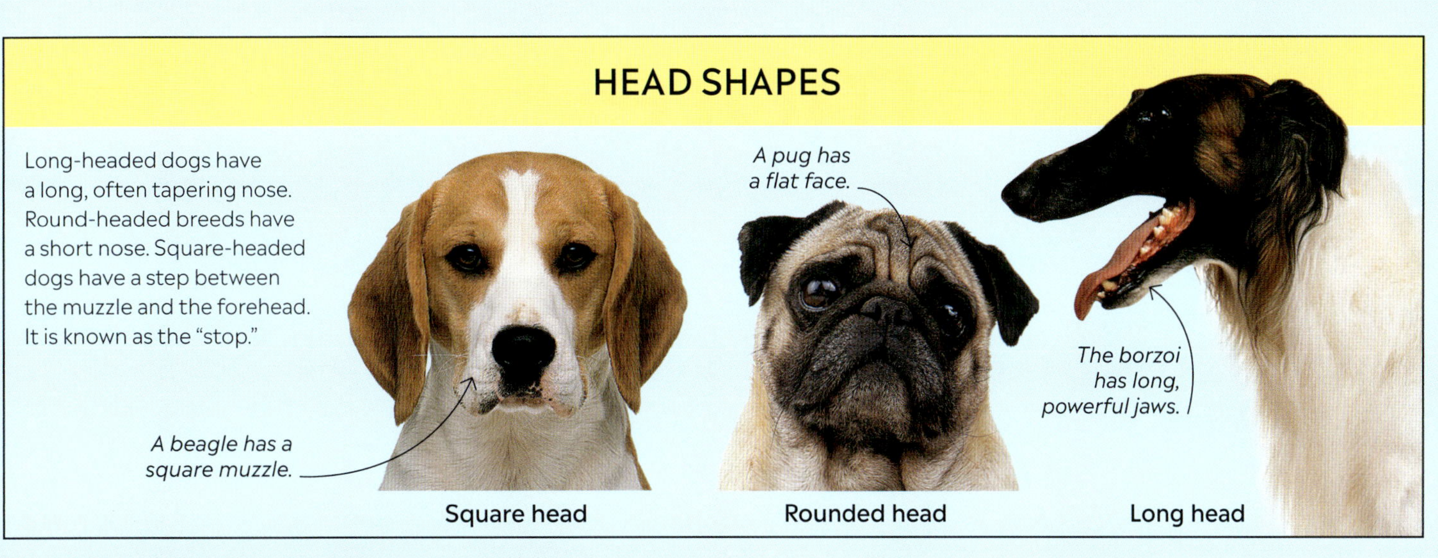

Herding dogs

Many dogs in this group still herd sheep and cattle today. They are active and intelligent. Most have a double coat, protecting them in rough weather.

The coat is mainly white.

Toy dogs

Also known as companion dogs, these breeds, mostly small in size, are intelligent and love attention.

Chihuahua

Terriers

Terriers are alert, bold, and fearless. Once kept as rat catchers, or to flush out foxes or badgers, they love digging.

Working dogs

This group includes guard dogs, such as the Doberman or mastiff; dogs to pull sleds or carts, such as the Siberian husky (seen in this photo) and Bernese mountain dog; and dogs working in search and rescue, such as the St. Bernard.

Find out **more**

One of the best ways of finding out more about dogs is to spend some time with them. You could walk a neighbor's dog or spend time with friends who have a dog. You could consider volunteering to help the Humane Society or the ASPCA.

A trainer teaches dog owners how to walk their dogs.

Dog training

Becoming a responsible pet owner is essential when you get a dog. Training schools teach dogs basic commands, and teach their humans how to communicate with their pets. You can search online, or call the nearest Kennel Club chapter in your area to find a suitable training school for your dog.

A pet dog

If you get a dog, it is important to spend time with it. As puppies, dogs need instructions on how to behave, but also support, affection, and praise.

Happy companions

The relationship between dogs and their humans can be a mutually beneficial and happy one. Dogs as pets are known to reduce anxiety, and long walks ensure that both dog and human get regular exercise and fresh air.

A rescue officer comforts a scared dog.

Help dogs in trouble

Help the Humane Society or the ASPCA, by giving time or money. Both rescue abandoned and mistreated animals.

The assistance dog provides warmth and affection as well as practical help.

Helpful dogs

Well-trained dogs can be a huge help to people with physical disabilities. The dogs open doors, pick up things, turn lights on and off, go for help, and provide constant companionship. Find out more about charities to see how you can help.

USEFUL WEBSITES

- Details about the American Kennel Club, information about dog breeds, and the AKC dog-training program: **www.akc.org**
- Learn about the process for adopting a pet from the ASPCA or for advice about caring for your pet: **www.aspca.org**
- Find out about the American Humane Society and the work they do: **www.americanhumane.org**
- Full coverage of the Westminster Dog Show: **www.westminsterkennelclub.org**
- Paws with a Cause trains assistance dogs for people with disabilities: **www.pawswithacause.org**

St. Bernard

PLACES TO VISIT

Westminster Kennel Dog Show, NY, NY
The show is held each February at Madison Square Garden. It features more than 2,500 dogs from 162 breeds competing to be "Best in Show."

National Dog Show, Philadelphia, PA
More than 2,500 dogs compete for Breed, Group, and "Best in Show" honors.

AKC Museum of the Dog, NY, NY
The museum houses one of the finest collections of art devoted to the dog.

Leeds Castle, Kent, UK
There is a collection of dog collars through the ages.

A dog collar from the collection at Leeds Castle, UK

Glossary

BAIT An edible item to attract animals.

BAT EARS Erect ears that are wide at the base, round at the tips, and point out.

BREED A group of dogs with particular characteristics or traits.

BREEDING The process of producing animals by mating one with another.

BREED STANDARD The official detail of a breed, setting out size, color, etc.

BRINDLE A mix of tan and black hair.

BRUSH A term used to describe a bushy tail; also a fox's tail.

Three cross-bred dogs

An Italian greyhound with her puppies

CAMOUFLAGE The coloration of an animal that blends in with the surroundings, or breaks up its outline with stripes or spots, making it harder to see.

CANID A member of the dog family; from *canis* (Latin for dog).

CANINE Dog or doglike; it is also the large tooth between the incisors and the premolars, used for gripping prey.

CARNIVORE A member of the order Carnivora, containing animals with specialized teeth for biting and shearing flesh. Most carnivores live on meat.

CROP The removal of the top of the ears so that they stand upright, and are pointed at the tip. Cropping is illegal in some countries.

CROSS-BREED An animal whose parents are from different breeds or who are cross-breeds.

DEN The retreat or resting place of a wild animal.

DEW CLAW The claw on the inside of the legs.

DEWLAP The loose folds of skin hanging under a dog's throat.

DOCK To remove an animal's tail, or part of it, by cutting. It is illegal in many countries today.

DOGGY-PADDLING To swim by moving your limbs in vertical circles, the way a dog swims.

DOMINANT The animal that is stronger and in a more powerful position in a group.

DOUBLE COAT A coat made up of a soft, insulating undercoat, through which longer guard hairs protrude.

DROP EARS Ears that hang down, close to the sides of the head.

ERECT Standing upright.

FAMILY Any of the taxonomic groups into which an order is divided. A family contains one or more genera. Canidae is the name of the dog family.

FERAL DOGS Domestic dogs, returned to the wild.

FORELEGS The two front legs.

GENUS (plural **GENERA**) Any of the taxonomic groups into which a family is divided. A genus contains one or more species.

GROOM To rub down and clean a dog.

GUARD HAIRS The coarse hairs that form the outer coat of some mammals.

HIND LEGS The back legs of a four-legged animal.

HOUNDS A group of hunting dogs, such as fast, lightly built "sight" hounds, and stocky, relentless "scent" hounds.

JAWS The part of the skull that frames the mouth and holds the teeth.

LIGAMENT The tough tissue that connects bones and cartilage, and that supports muscle.

Labradors are sporting dogs.

LITTER A group of puppies born at one time to one female.

MONGREL A dog of mixed or unknown breeding. Also known as cross-bred dogs.

MOLT To lose hair so that new growth can take place. Some dogs molt their thick, winter coat in the spring.

MUSCLE Tissue that can contract or relax, and as a result, allow movement.

MUZZLE The part of the head that is in front of the eyes.

A Bichon Frise has a curly coat.

NON-SPORTING DOGS A group of breeds that haven't been sorted into the other groups (hounds, terriers, sporting, herding, working, and toy dogs).

OMNIVORE An animal that eats both plants and meat.

PACK A group of animals of the same kind that usually live together, may be related, and hunt together.

PEDIGREE The record of a pure-breed dog's ancestors.

PUPPY A dog less than one year old.

PURE-BREED A dog with parents of the same breed. Also, a pedigree dog.

REGURGITATE To bring up food that has been eaten. Wolves do this to feed their young.

RUFF Long, thick hair around the neck.

SADDLE Black markings in the shape and position of the saddle on a horse.

SCAVENGER An animal that feeds on animal remains that it steals or finds.

SCENT HOUND A dog that has been bred to use its excellent sense of smell more than its sight or hearing when pursuing other animals, such as bloodhounds, beagles, and foxhounds.

SELECTIVE BREEDING When humans control the breeding of animals for specific features, such as head shape or sharp eyesight. If the breeding is not supervised, such characteristics can be lost.

SIGHT HOUND A dog with excellent sight that will chase game while it can see it, such as greyhounds, Irish wolfhounds, and borzoi.

SKELETON The framework of bones that gives shape to an animal, provides anchorage for muscles, protects vital organs, is a source of blood cells, and provides a mineral store.

SPECIES Any of the taxonomic groups into which a genus is divided. Members of the same species are able to breed with each other. All dogs are the same species and can mate with each other.

SPITZ Any of various breeds of dog characterized by a stocky build, a curled tail, a pointed muzzle, and erect ears. The chow chow is a spitz.

SPORTING DOGS A group of dogs trained to work with a hunter at pointing, flushing out, and retrieving game.

STEREOSCOPIC VISION The ability to see a slightly different picture with each eye, and, by putting them together, to judge distances accurately.

SUCKLE To suck milk from the mother. The term also means to give milk to a young animal.

TAPETUM LUCIDUM The cells at the back of a dog's eye that reflect light; it makes it possible for a dog to see well when there is not a lot of light.

TENDON A band of tough tissue that attaches a muscle to a bone.

TERRIERS A group of active, inquisitive dogs originally trained to hunt for animals by digging under the ground. Their name comes from *terra*, which means "earth" in Latin. Scotties, Airedales, and fox terriers are a few examples of this breed.

Yorkshire terrier

THIRD EYELID A thin fold of skin in the upper and lower eyelids; it can be drawn across the eye to protect it from dirt. It is also called the nictitating membrane.

TOY DOGS A group of very small dogs that are popular as pets.

UNDERCOAT (or **UNDERFUR**) A dense, soft fur beneath the outer, coarser fur in some mammals.

WEAN To cause a puppy to replace its mother's milk with other food.

WOMB An internal organ that houses a growing baby.

WORKING DOGS A group of dogs that work for people, such as by pulling sleds or herding sheep.

Poodle

Index

Acknowledgments

The publisher would like to thank the following people for their help with making the book: Taiyaba Khatoon, Priya Singh, Manpreet Kaur, and SamRajkumar for picture research; Binta Jallow, Bipasha Roy, and Vandana Likhmania for editorial assistance; Hazel Beynon for proofreading; and Elizabeth Wise for the index.

The publisher would like to thank the following for their kind permission to reproduce their photographs:

(Key: a-above; b-below/bottom; c-center; f-far; l-left; r-right; t-top)

Adobe Stock: ajayptp 36clb, Chris Brignell 42cr, Evelyn 9tr, jose 4crb, 15bc, Sebastian Kaulitzki 11bl, Sonja 32cl; **Sunday Agbonika:** 46bl; **Alamy Stock Photo:** AB Forces News Collection 47tr, Artepics 41tc, Arterra Picture Library / De Meester Johan 46-47, Arterra Picture Library / van der Meer Marica 43tl, ARTGEN 48tr, 48bl, Avalon / Bruce Coleman Inc / Leonard L. Rue III 25cr, Tristan Barrington 23bl, Chronicle 50bc, 53tr, 58cr, Connect Images / Simon Murrell 62tl, Simon Curtis 4tr, 58tr, Alvise Armellini / dpa 35cl, dpa picture alliance 29br, EnVogue_Photo / Cernan Elias 66bl, Farlap 66cl, Florilegius 9clb, FLPA 37tr, Eddie Gerald 35crb, Chris Hellier 61tr, Peter Horree 34br, Janet Horton 60b, Image Source Limited / Radius Images 21tl, imageBROKER / Ronald Wittek 20bl, imageBROKER.com / Michael Weber 23tr, imageBROKER.com / Stefan Wackerhagen 57bl, imageBROKER.com / Thomas Sbampato 22bl, INTERFOTO / History 49cl, Ernie Janes 56cla, Ronald Wilfred Jansen 19tl, Glenn Larsen 42cl, Logic Images 22br, mauritius images GmbH / Reinhard Eisele 67b, Jim Brandenburg / Minden Pictures 23cla, Roland Seitre / Minden Pictures 37clb, Nature Picture Library / Luke Massey 33bl, North Wind Picture Archives 29tl, Papilio / Jack Milchanowski 22-23c, piemags / ww2archive 52tr, Prisma by Dukas Presseagentur GmbH / Van der Meer Rene 35c, 69br, Olaf Protze 3br, 44br, R.M.TONEGUZZO 56cr, Paul Sawer 28l, Kevin Schafer 32c, Adrian Sherratt 69tl, Skimage 59tc, Geoff Smith 42tl, The Picture Art Collection 60crb, The Print Collector / © CM Dixon / Heritage Images 36tr, Tierfotoagentur / S. Starick 56b, Ann and Steve Toon 21tr, E.D. Torial 68cla, UPI / Bill Greenblatt 46bc, Grossemy Vanessa 13tl, Alan Dyer / VWPics 8tr, Claudia Wiens 36br, World History Archive 44tr, Natallia Yaumenenka 62cl; **Ardea:** Jean-Paul Ferrero 22-23t, Kenneth W Fink 31tl; **Bridgeman Images:** 7tl, 19cl, © Ditz. All Rights Reserved 2025 6cl, Look and Learn / Illustrated Papers Collection 52cr, Photo © John Noott Galleries, Broadway, Worcestershire, UK 41tl; © **The Trustees of the British Museum. All rights reserved:** 26crb; **Depositphotos Inc:** evrmmnt 4br, 68tr, focusandblur 62c, lifeonwhite 4bl, 59tl; **Shirin Dhabhar:** 18tr; **Dorling Kindersley:** 14cr, 27tr, 38clb, 38cb, Tracy Morgan: J.P. & C.Smith; Anderson 66cb, (c) The Trustees of the British Museum. All Rights 61tl, (c) The Trustees of the British Museum. All Rights Reserved 14tr, 25br, 34tr, 34crb, 35tr, 35bl, 40cr, Tracy Morgan: J.Gostynska 64bl, Colin Keates / Natural History Museum, London 2bl, 4cla, 8c, 8cb, 8bc, 9cla, 10cb, 10bl, 10-11c, 11tl, 11tr, 13cla, 13bl, 29cr, Tracy Morgan 12cra, 17tc, 65br, 66bc, Tracy Morgan: S.Dunning 70cl, Tracy Morgan / J.P. Wood 67cra, Jerry Young 1, 2tl, 2tr, 2c, 2-3b, 3cb, 4cra, 4clb, 6cb, 6bl, 6-7c, 7c, 10tr, 10c, 10clb, 12ca, 12c, 12cr, 12crb, 13tr, 13br, 14cla, 14br, 17tr, 17cr, 18b, 20cl, 20c, 21cl, 24-25, 26tr, 26cra, 26cl, 26bl, 26br, 27, 27tl, 28cb, 29cl, 30clb, 31tr, 31cl, 32b, 33, 33cl, 37, 37tl, 38-39b, 44-45, 50ca, 50clb, 52c, 55c, 58b, 60c, 63tr, 63cra, 63cr, 63cb; **Dreamstime.com:** Alexandragl 14clb, Beritk 36cl, Danica Chang 67cla, Nick Dale 24cl, Designvectorpro 9crb (greyhound), Dima1970 9crb (spaniel), 9crb (toy dog), 9bc, 9bc (spitz), 9br, Eriklam 38cl, Chris Fourie 25tl, Vlad Ghiea 28br, Guruxox 62bc, David Havel 13clb, Isselee 3tl, 45tr, Luboslav Ivanko 44bl, Sebastian Kaulitzki 11br, Mykhailo Kazaryk 62c (4), Elena Ladanovskaya 15tl, Sergey Lavrentev / Laures 71tr, Lynnealbright 62bl, Igor Mojzes 68b, Anastasiia Neibauer 9crb (Feral), Denis Pepin 25tr, Dario Lo Presti 35tl, Marco Antonio Rodriguez Rodriguez 9cb (x7), Gabriel Rojo 4tl, 32tr, SaveJungle 9crb, Natallia Yaumenenka 62-63, 71br; **Getty Images:** 500Px Plus / Daniel Parent 30-31b, Markus Platzbecker / 500px 50-51, BLOOMimage / SAKIstyle 12clb, Corbis Documentary / Tom Nebbia 64c, Corbis Historical / Gregory Smith 65bl, De Agostini / DEA / A. Dagli Orti 40cl, imageBROKER / Verena Scholze 42clb, Moment / Oscar Wong 47br, Werner Forman / Universal Images Group 24bl, 34bl, 41tr; **Getty Images / iStock:** Antic Zlatko 63tc, CathyDoi 15, Cavan Images 39tl, DamianKuzdak 11cr, E+ / Drazen_ 42b, E+ / O2O Creative 69tr, Ohoho 52cl, Seregraff 12cla, SteveOehlenschlager 51br, tarasov_vl 19r, Sue Thatcher 53tc; **Alexandra Horowitz:** Vegar Abelsnes 17br; **Jaikla:** Ittikorn Thepmani 63br; **Courtesy National Gallery of Art, Washington:** Paul Mellon Collection 55bl; **Dr. Angela Perri:** 9tc; **ResearchGate:** Morey, Darcy. (1994). The Early Evolution of the Domestic Dog. American Scientist - AMER SCI. 82. 336-347. 10.2307 / 29775234. 9br (Modern Evolution); **Reuters:** Lisi Niesner 30cra; **Saint Louis Art Museum:** Gift of J. Lionberger Davis 40tl; **Shutterstock.com:** Vickey Chauhan 7br, hedgehog94 46tl, New Africa 46c; **Claudio Sillero:** Dr Jorgelina Marino 23br; **Alain Thomas:** 39tr

Cover images: *Front:* **Dorling Kindersley:** (c) The Trustees of the British Museum. All Rights Reserved crb, Jerry Young cra, bl; **Dreamstime.com:** 9dreamstudio cr/ (bone), Mdorottya cl, Peter Zijlstra cla/ (toy); **Getty Images / iStock:** E+ / mehmettorlak cla, Liliboas clb, MirasWonderland c; *Back*: **Dorling Kindersley:** (c) The Trustees of the British Museum. All Rights Reserved cla; **Shutterstock.com:** Bigzumi cra; *Spine*: **Getty Images / iStock:** MirasWonderland.